To _____

From _____   _____

GW01557954

Bedtime Prayers for Little Ones

Published by Garborg's Heart 'n Home, Inc.
P.O. Box 20132, Bloomington, MN 55420

SPCN 5-5044-0054-6

January 1

God, I'm ready to have You do something new in my life this year. Thanks for leading me. I'm ready to follow!

December 31

Jesus, guess what? Tomorrow starts a brand new year. I'll be one year older next year, and I pray that I'll be one year closer to You.

January 2

God, You're so big and my voice is so small. I don't understand how You hear me, but I'm sure glad you do.

December 30

It's been great praying to You every night like this, Lord. Prayer has made a big difference in my life this year, and I want to keep praying all through the next year. Thanks for prayer.

January 3

Thank You for all the important people who helped You write Your message so that it could come to me in the Bible. Every time I read my Bible, it's like getting a letter from You. I love getting mail!

December 29

Sometimes I don't want to share my things, God. Like new toys. Help me to remember that You want me to share. That's important because I want to be like You.

January 4

I love it when my best friend and I get to spend a whole day together. That must be how You feel when Your friends come and spend time with You. I want to be Your friend!

December 28

Thank You that You've kept my family and friends safe all through this year. God bless all my family and friends.

January 5

I love our country, Lord, and I love our flag. It's really pretty. Please help the people in our country live in peace, and help them to know You.

December 27

Inside I feel so peaceful tonight, God. Even though Christmas is over, I still have Your joy inside. For Christians, the joy of Christmas can last all year. I'm glad for that!

January 6

God, I need Your help. I want to tell my friends about You, but I'm stuck for an idea. I'm going to be quiet for a moment. Please help me to think of a good way to tell my friends how much You love them.

December 26

I didn't get everything I
wanted for Christmas,
Lord. But I'm really happy
with what I did get.
Thanks for the people
who love me and
gave me the gifts.

January 7

Grandmothers and grandfathers really need somebody to watch out for them. Would You please do that, Lord? Please make a note to especially care tonight for everyone who has white hair and wrinkles.

December 25

Happy Birthday, Lord Jesus!
If You had candles to blow
out on a cake and a wish
to make, I think it would
be that all the people
in the world would
come to know You!

January 8

Jesus, thank You for being so kind. You take care of everything, even the little animals in the forest. Thank You for taking care of me.

December 24

Jesus, I'm sorry that the innkeeper didn't have enough room for You in his inn. I have room for You in my heart.

January 9

I don't understand how God can be my Father and also be Jesus and even the Holy Spirit. But You know what? I don't have to understand. All I have to do is love You.

December 23

I have a favorite Christmas carol that I'm thinking of tonight, Lord. Would You like to hear me sing it to You? Okay, here goes....

January 10

I like music a lot, Lord!
I have a lot of favorite songs
to sing. I'm glad You made
it so people can sing
together. My favorite
song is _____.

December 22

Of all the miracles You ever performed, I think the greatest miracle of all is that You, our great big God who created the universe, became a baby. I wonder how You did that! I don't need to know. I'm just glad that You came.

January 11

Snow is so white and clean. I can see why You sometimes like to cover up the earth with snow. When You forgive me for my sins, it feels like being covered up with snow. It makes me feel clean inside.

December 21

I pray for people in wheelchairs who may have a hard time getting out and going shopping. I pray that their friends and neighbors will help them.

January 12

I just want You to know that I think one of Your very best ideas is friends. I love my friends. If I tell You the names of my best friends, will You bless them in a special way? Well, here they are....

December 20

I pray for blind people who can't see the twinkling lights and starry nights. It's neat to think that the first thing that blind people who believe in You will see when they get to heaven is...You!

January 13

Jesus, I just wish I could hug You tonight, but since I can't do that, show me someone I can hug tomorrow as if it were You.

December 19

I pray for deaf people who can't hear all the beautiful music this time of year. It's neat to think that the first thing deaf people who believe in You will hear when they go to heaven is a great big choir of angels.

January 14

Africa is a big place where many people are hungry and suffering from famine. Please help the missionaries to find food for these people, Jesus.

December 18

Jesus, I'm going to look outside for a star right now. I pray for other boys or girls who are looking at the same star tonight, that they would know that You made it.

January 15

When am I ever going to grow up, Lord? I wish I could do stuff grownups do...like staying up late. Help me to be patient and enjoy being a kid.

December 17

Sometimes I get angry for no reason and I have a hard time feeling like I want to pray to You. Please help me to give those feelings to You and make my heart right so I can pray to You...and mean everything I say.

January 16

Once in a while I see Mom or Dad feeling sad. It doesn't make me feel good, but I guess they have feelings, too. Help me cheer them up when they're feeling sad.

December 16

Jesus, a lot of people feel really lonely this time of year because they don't have a family to celebrate Christmas with. Please reach out to lonely people and let them know that You love them.

January 17

Jesus, I don't like it when I say something stupid and the other kids laugh at me. Help me to remember what You did when people laughed at You. You didn't get mad, You just forgave them.

December 15

Once in a while my mom or dad asks me to do something that I don't think is cool—like take an umbrella or wear a hat. Lord, help me to do it without complaining. Thanks for parents who watch out for me.

January 18

Lord, it says You taught the teachers in the Temple when You were only twelve. You must have really enjoyed being in church to worship Your Father. I like being in church, too! Thank You for my church.

December 14

Jesus, You probably never tasted a Christmas cookie when You lived on earth. They sure are good! I like the kind shaped like little trees and stars with red and green sprinkles on top. Hurray for cookies!

January 19

When I hear You say "Follow Me," I want to look at following You like You do—an adventure!

December 13

I have a lot of my own reasons to praise You, God. Would You like to hear them? Here they are....

January 20

Tonight I want to pray for the leader of our country and all the important people who help him make decisions. Please guide him, Jesus.

December 12

Please bless all the mail carriers who will deliver Christmas cards tomorrow. Their bags must be jam-packed full of cards! Help them to deliver the many cards to the right people. I like Christmas cards, and I am thankful for our mail carrier.

January 21

Why did You make funny bones? I'm sure they are good for something—just like everything else You made. Thank You for making all the parts of my body (even the parts I don't understand, like funny bones).

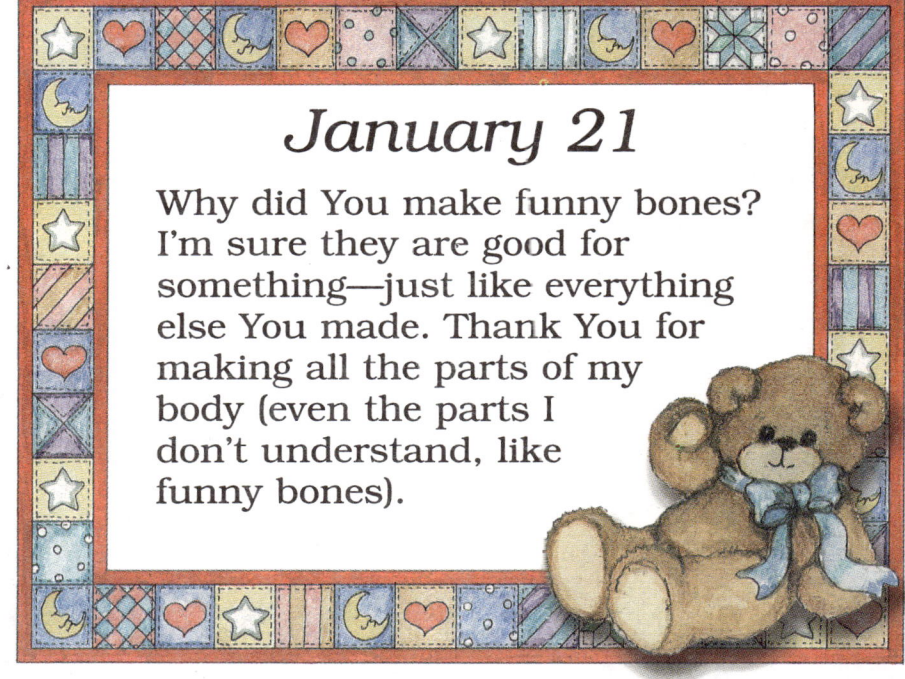

December 11

I like the song that goes, "Silent Night, Holy Night... all is calm, all is bright." That's how I feel tonight, Lord. Thank You for making me calm and silent on the inside.

January 22

Sometimes I forget how good You are, God. Would you help me to remember that You want the very best for me?

December 10

Tomorrow I want to draw
You a picture of all the
things I like about
wintertime. Thank You
for this beautiful time
of year.

January 23

Lord, help me to find someone to say "God bless you" to tomorrow. (Sneezes don't count!)

December 9

God, why is snow so wonderful?
Maybe because it covers things
up. The Bible says You cover up
our sins just like snow covers
the ground. Snow makes
the world look peaceful....
You make me feel
peaceful.

January 24

Lord, I'm going to tell You
about someone who is sick.
I'd like You to make him well.
But if he isn't going to get
well right away, would
You let him know that
You are there to help
him? Thanks!

December 8

Lord, there's a cold place called Iceland way up north. Polar bears live there...and people do, too. Help them to be warm tonight. And help them to know You love them.

January 25

I'm glad You made puppies and kittens, baby horses and bunnies, Lord. They remind me that You really love small things. Like me!

December 7

It seems like it will take forever for Christmas to get here. Help me to be patient and to find lots of things to do to keep my mind off how far away it is.

January 26

God, You're better than a collection of a gazillion stickers. You're also better than a kitchen full of all my favorite things to eat (and sometimes that's Fruit Loops and Fritos).

December 6

People are crowding into all the shopping malls right now, God. They are busy buying things for Christmas. Help them to focus not so much on things...but on You!

January 27

Lord, thank You for angels. I'm glad You have angels watching over me and my family. It's neat to think I'll meet those angels one day when we all go to heaven. Tell them thanks for helping!

December 5

Jesus, I just want to tell You tonight that I love You. So let me say it out loud right now in my own words....

January 28

Lord, sometimes I feel like
I'm empty on the inside.
I want to believe in You in
a bigger way. Tonight,
would You fill me up
on the inside?

December 4

I get all jumpy inside, Lord,
when I see twinkling lights and
hear Christmas bells and listen
to carols and go outside and
play in the snow. This is
the best time of year. I'm
glad that You made
Christmas! Thank You
for your birthday.

January 29

Lord, turn the sad things of my life into something joyful. You did it with Jesus and His cross... thank You for doing it in me.

December 3

God, I think it's interesting that You made people in different colors and shapes and sizes. It would be really boring if we all looked the same. Help everybody to appreciate the differences.

January 30

God, help grownups to understand that kids like me can love just like they can. When I give a grownup a hug tomorrow, I'll say it's from You.

December 2

Lord, lots of Jewish people are celebrating Hanukkah this week. I pray that You will help our Jewish friends and neighbors to know Jesus in a special and personal way.

January 31

If I see a stop sign tomorrow, Lord, would you help me to stop and think of You?

December 1

Christmas is coming! Lord, help me not to think so much about getting gifts, but giving them. You said in the Bible that it's more blessed to give than to receive.

February 1

Dear God, I have something to say tonight: You're awesome!

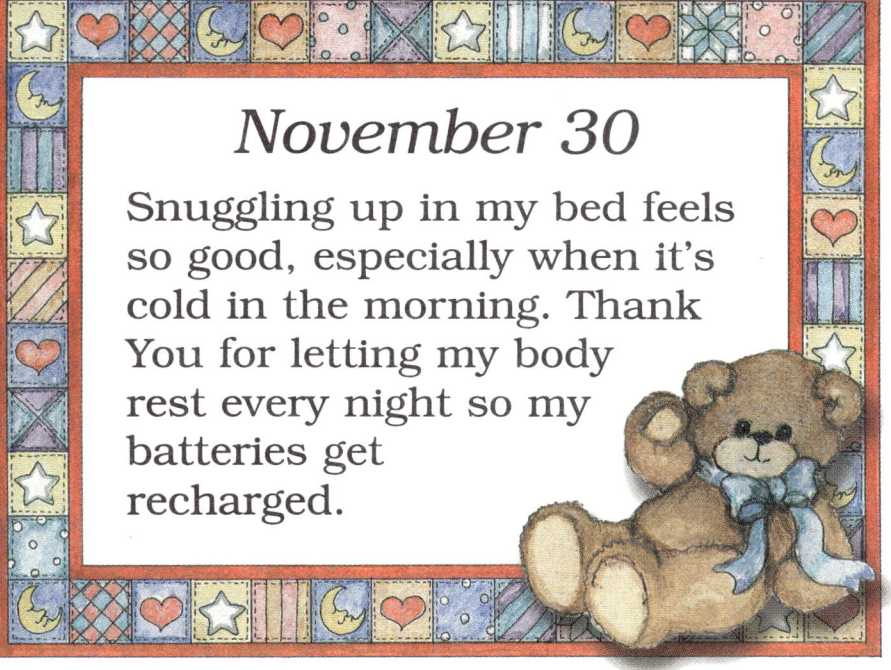

November 30

Snuggling up in my bed feels so good, especially when it's cold in the morning. Thank You for letting my body rest every night so my batteries get recharged.

February 2

Sometimes I feel really shy when I pray. You're a big King and I'm a little kid. Help me to remember that I'm a child of the King.

November 29

November is almost over,
Lord. Wow, did this month
go fast! Psalm 90:12 says,
"Teach me to number
my days." Help me to
make each day
count for You.

February 3

You know that there are lots of homeless people in the cities, don't You, Lord? It's awfully cold on the streets at night. Please help them to find shelter. And help the workers in rescue missions to provide beds and blankets.

November 28

Lord, I pray that people would stop making violent cartoons for television. I don't want to see cartoon characters fighting and hurting each other, even if it is pretend. I pray they would make good things for kids to watch.

February 4

What's the funniest joke
You've ever heard, Lord?
The Bible says that
You laugh. I'd like
to hear what that
sounds like.

November 27

Sometimes I have so many questions about zillions of things. God, I'm glad that the really important answers are in Your big answer book, the Bible!

February 5

Sometimes I say things I shouldn't say, Lord. Please forgive me and remind me the next time that words can hurt other kids.

November 26

Lord, You care so much for orphans. Please help us to find mothers and fathers to adopt all of the orphans.

February 6

Sometimes I feel like moving far away, Lord. Other days I don't ever want to move. Help me to be happy wherever I am.

November 25

Thank You for boots and scarves and mittens. It's fun getting all bundled up to go out in the cold. I especially like it when I can come inside after playing and feel the warmth of our home.

February 7

I daydream a lot, Lord.
Is that okay? I hope
I dream of things
You like.

November 24

Thank You for all the people who care for me. I'm so glad that kids have grownups to love them!

February 8

Teachers have a very important job because they teach little kids like me. I pray for the teachers to be kind and wise. Thank you for teachers.

November 23

Jesus, I don't think they made pumpkin pie when You were a little boy. It tastes great. Especially with whipped cream! Thank You for teaching people how to make pumpkin pie.

February 9

Help me to remember, God,
that prayer is not only talking
to You...but being quiet so
that I can hear You talk back
to me. (I like it when You
put Your thoughts in
my mind.)

November 22

I feel really good when I tell You "thank You." Thank You for all the things You give us. Most of all, thank You, God, for being...You. You are wonderful!

February 10

God, there are little kids like me all over the world who are asking You to come into their hearts. I want You in my heart, too. I want it to be Your home.

November 21

You make food taste so good, God. Thank You for turkey and stuffing and mashed potatoes and gravy (that's the best part). Thank You for our food.

February 11

Tonight I want to thank You for dying on the cross for me. Thank You for thinking of me when You were on Your cross.

November 20

Lord, I pray for the city rescue missions and soup kitchens that are feeding many homeless people. Help the homeless people to know they have lots of friends who care.

February 12

My pastor works really hard, Lord. Please bless him—I hope he will be our pastor for a long time.

November 19

When I go to church this weekend, Lord, I want to show You that I love You with all of my heart. Teach me how to worship You.

February 13

Jesus, when You were a little boy, did it ever snow in Your town? I think snow is one of the neatest things You made. People do fun things in the snow like sledding and making snowmen and even snow angels. Thanks for snow!

November 18

My bedroom is my own very special, private place. Thank You for the clothes in my closet and the books on my shelf and the toys in my chest. These are wonderful bedroom things and I thank You for them.

February 14

Today was Valentine's Day, Lord, and people were giving lots of cards with hearts. Help them to know that You love them no matter how many Valentines they get.

November 17

It feels so good to win at something, Lord...a game, a race, a contest. Is that what will heaven be like? Winning all the time? I pray for the people who have never won anything. I pray that they would get to go to heaven and be winners!

February 15

Lord, sometimes I'm afraid something bad might happen to someone I love (and need). Would You please chase those fears away?

November 16

God, last night I talked about
how You made the earth in just
seven days. Now I'm thinking
about how long it's taking You
to make a place in heaven
for me. If earth is this
neat, I can't imagine
what heaven's like!

February 16

I love the smell of warm pies, hot chocolate, and _____. Thanks for my nose, Lord...even when it runs.

November 15

God, You created everything in just seven days. That's a lot of work in just a little bit of time! Would You please help my parents with the work they have to do?

February 17

War is terrible, God. People get hurt and even die in war. When I fight, Mom sends me to my room. I wish You could do the same with those countries that are fighting each other. I pray for the fighting to stop.

November 14

Lord, I want to pray for my Sunday School teacher tonight. Please help my teacher to be the best teacher ever, and help me to listen so that I can learn all about Your wonderful world.

February 18

February means that the sky is gray, the trees are bare, and the lawn is brown. But that's okay, Lord. I can see Your beauty all year 'round.

November 13

Sometimes when it's cold, I need extra blankets on my bed, Lord. And sometimes when I'm feeling cold and lonely, I need extra love. Thank You that Your love is the biggest, best blanket ever!

February 19

Friends are neat. They'll pick you first when choosing sides in a game, they'll invite you over when their dog has pups, and they'll be proud of you when you do a good job. Thanks for friends, God. They're great!

November 12

I love to hear wind chimes when the wind blows. It's such a happy sound and it makes me feel all tingly inside. Thank You for the wind on a starry November night like this.

February 20

Tonight I want to pray for all the important people who run our town. I don't know all their names, Lord, but You do. Help them to make good decisions.

November 11

Every time a baby is born, it's a miracle. Help people to value the life of each little baby. I pray that all the unborn babies inside their mommies will be safe.

February 21

It's amazing that You, Jesus, became man. It's neat to think that You were a kid who tied shoelaces on Your sandals and threw pebbles in streams and sat around a fire at night. You're so...real!

November 10

Lord, every single person was created by You. You created people to love You and enjoy You. Lots of people don't know that. Help all those in my town to love You, Lord...that's the only way they'll have joy!

February 22

Jesus, did You have chores when You were a kid? It seems like I have a lot. Help me to get them done so that I can have lots of time to play with my friends.

November 9

Holy Spirit, I'm so glad that You are living and working in the world today, especially in the hearts of Christians. Thank You for working in my heart. In fact...would You please do more work in my heart?

February 23

It's neat being a brother or a sister to another kid. And, Jesus, I'm so glad that You are like a big older brother who is the wisest, bravest, kindest, best brother a kid could have.

November 8

Japan is a little country. Many of the people who live there spend a lot of time working. God, please help people in Japan to take time to get to know and love You. Please bless the children who live there.

February 24

I'm glad that heaven's not a place where we're going to spend our time playing harps and polishing gold. You have better things for us to do. Thank You, Lord, for taking all of eternity to think up exciting stuff for us to do.

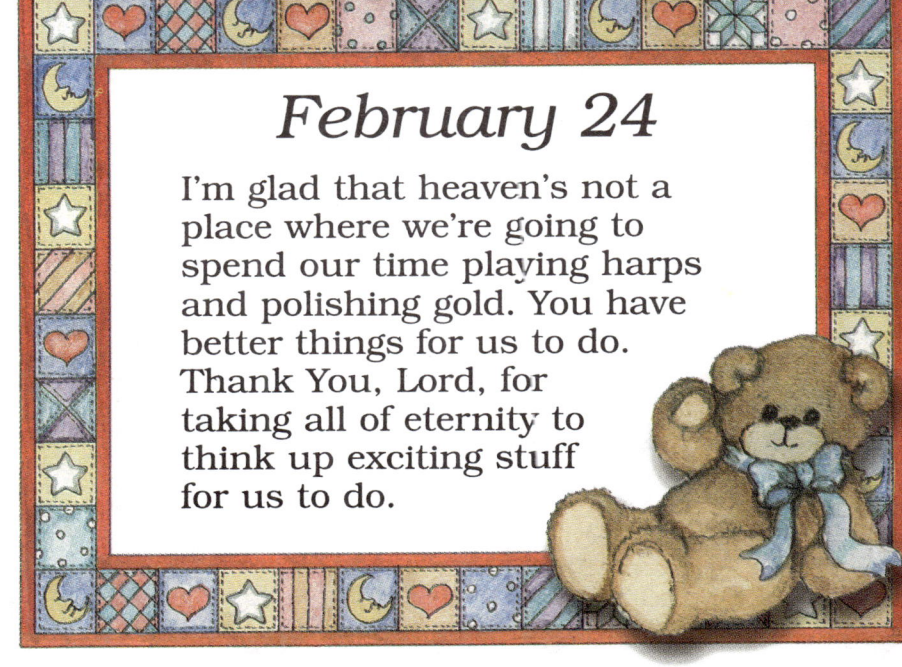

November 7

Jesus, would You please send a couple of big angels to stand guard around my bed tonight? Please have them chase away any scary thoughts I might have or any nightmares. Thank You that angels obey You!

February 25

Lord, thank You for making goldfish and hamsters and parakeets for kids to be friends with. It's like You made those animals just for...kids!

November 6

Lord, I love it when I'm in bed and see a little bit of light in the hallway. It reminds me that someone is caring for me and watching over me. That's why I like it when when people call You the Light of the World. Thank You for loving and watching over us.

February 26

There's a country way far away called India where many people don't believe in You, Lord. They believe in little gods made of stone and wood. Please help the missionaries there as they talk about You to the people.

November 5

Help me to see myself as
You see me: terrific!

February 27

Lord, I'm sorry I complain about vegetables, but You have to admit they don't taste as good as some of the other food you made! Thank You for all kinds of food... lima beans as well as pizza.

November 4

Lord, governments all around the world are trying to make peace, and they're not doing a very good job of it. Help them to ask You for help because Your peace is the only kind of peace that lasts.

February 28

Jesus, there's a kid in our neighborhood that no one seems to like. Help me to be brave enough to do something nice for that kid.

November 3

I have wonderful aunts, Lord. I thank You for giving them to me. I want to tell You how much I love my aunts right now so that You will bless them in a big way.

February 29

I'm glad I don't have to use a lot of fancy words in my prayers, God. Thanks for hearing what I say, no matter how I say it!

November 2

Lord, once in a while I get jealous of things other kids have. Help me to be thankful for what You have given me.

March 1

I like to think about how big and strong and mighty You are. It makes me feel safe!

November 1

When I look up at the stars
at night, it almost looks
like the sky is on fire. It's
fantastic to think that
one day I'll be up
there with You.

March 2

Lord, I'm so glad that Spring isn't far away. I can't wait to see leaves on the trees, flowers in the fields, and birds in the back yard. Thank You, Lord, that Spring is coming soon.

October 31

I pray that people around the world will stop believing in false gods. I pray that they will believe in You, the only true God.

March 3

Lord, does everyone have crazy ideas like me? Help me use my imagination to do neat things for You.

October 30

Lord, tomorrow is Halloween. It's a time when some people dress up in scary costumes and do things You don't like. Thank You that You're strong enough to keep us safe from anything.

March 4

I have a problem, Jesus, and I don't know how to fix it. Would You please help me to solve it? I'll be quiet in my heart so I can hear You answer.

October 29

Jesus, You told me in Matthew
5:14, "You are the light of the
world." I want to be Your light.
Not a little light like a match
that's on fire only for a
second, but a warm light
that keeps on glowing,
like a candle. Help me
to shine for You.

March 5

Lord, do You want me to be a missionary someday? I don't need to know right now. I guess I just want to tell You that anything you want me to be would be okay with me.

October 28

Lord, how many hairs do I have on my head? You must care about me a lot if You know that much about me. It makes me feel important. I want to thank You tonight for caring so much.

March 6

I don't like it when other kids use my things without asking me. Help me not to be selfish, Lord, and help me to remember to ask before taking. Thank You.

October 27

Lord, heaven is being where You are forever. Hell is being away from You forever. I have a choice and I choose... heaven! Thank You for helping me to choose You and Your big wide wonderful heaven.

March 7

I like the story You told about
the Good Samaritan, Lord.
He helped someone who was
hurting. If I see someone
who is hurting tomorrow,
would You remind
me to be a good
samaritan, too?

October 26

I thank You for chores, Lord. Chores teach me how to be helpful and responsible. Tomorrow, help me to do my chores with a smile.

March 8

It's hard to imagine how You can see everything in the universe all at the same time, God. But You can! Help me to remember this the next time I feel like getting into trouble.

October 25

I like the story of the Prodigal Son, Lord. It's neat to think that his father welcomed him home with such a big party. One day You will welcome us home, and, boy, what a party that is going to be! Thank You for being such a wonderful Father.

March 9

Lord, I want to memorize a Bible verse tomorrow. Help me to find a verse I can memorize. (Only please, Lord, make it short!)

October 24

Lord, I want to be a better listener so I can learn things. My parents have so many wonderful things they want to teach me.

March 10

I don't understand why my parents say "no" sometimes. Teach me to trust them and believe that what they say is best for me.

October 23

I like to fold my hands,
bow my head, and close
my eyes when I pray. I do
this to show You how
much I honor You,
God. I love You and
I respect You.

March 11

I pray for Sunday School teachers in my church, Lord. They work hard every week and take time just for us. Give them all a hug tonight.

October 22

You have so many wonderful names—Savior, King of Kings, the Good Shepherd, and Lord. There must be so many names because it's impossible to find just one that describes how fantastic You are. My favorite name for You is _____.

March 12

Thank You for scary stuff like snakes, spiders, and lightning. Those things remind me that You're the one who keeps me safe.

October 21

Squash is a silly name for a vegetable, but I'm sure glad You invented it. It comes in all kinds of funny shapes and colors. I'm learning to like squash, God. You are so good to make so many different kinds of vegetables.

March 13

Lord, it's scary when I hear people yelling at each other. Help people to obey You because You are the Prince of Peace... and Quiet.

October 20

Lord, Mexico is a very poor country and the people there really need our prayers. I pray for little kids who live in villages way up in the mountains. Help them to know You, Lord.

March 14

Lord, teach me to get
excited about something
I do well without bragging
about it. I want to
learn what it means
to be humble.

October 19

It's fun to jump in a big pile of leaves. It's even fun to rake them up. I like it when work is fun! Thank You for giving me work to do.

March 15

When my mom hugs me or my teacher smiles at me, it makes me feel warm and special. God, I can't hug You, but here's my heart. I love You!

October 18

Thank You, God, for giving me a nice home and good food and a family. Thank you, too, for giving me a fun day and keeping me safe.

March 16

Some kids believe that monsters live under their beds. I know that's not true, but sometimes I'm still scared of the dark. Help me to remember that You're right here next to me making everything light and bright.

October 17

Jesus, the Bible tells us
about a lot of miracles that
You did. My favorite is the
time that You _____.
Thank You that You
work miracles in
my life, too.

March 17

The Ten Commandments are Your rules for us so that we can love You, help others, and be happy. One of the commandments says, "Honor your father and mother." Teach me how to do that, Lord.

October 16

I have a friend who needs to know You, Lord. Would You please take care of this friend? Thank You for loving all of us, God.

March 18

It feels so good after I've
told You that I'm sorry for
something I did wrong.
I feel all clean inside.
Your forgiveness is
so good.

October 15

I like things that are orange, God. Like the orange leaves on trees. And orange Lifesavers. And pumpkins! Thank You for making this season so orange.

March 19

Just in case no one else in
the whole wide world has
said this to You today,
Lord, I want to say it
to You right now:
I love You!

October 14

Tonight I pray for the school bus drivers who take kids to school. The drivers have a big responsibility. Help them to drive safely so kids can arrive at school safe and sound.

March 20

Jesus, it seems like summer vacation will never come. Please help me to be full of summertime joy even on boring winter days.

October 13

Lord, I think it's neat that You call us Your sheep. I like it that You are my Shepherd. Thanks for taking care of me, just as if I were one of Your lambs.

March 21

God, the Bible says You made everything. That's a lot of stuff to have to keep track of! Thanks for watching over my family and me.

October 12

I love swing sets! Thanks for all the neat things on them like seesaws and monkey bars and slides and swings. God, thanks for making fun stuff!

March 22

Lord, the Bible says there's a special angel watching over me. What does he look like? What's his name? I can't wait to meet him someday. (Or maybe it's a girl angel?!)

October 11

Lord, sometimes I can't think of a way to tell my mom and dad what I feel inside. There's so much I want to say, but I can't get it out. Please help me to learn new words, so I can explain how I feel.

March 23

God, there are kids in this world who people call retarded. But You call them Your children just like I'm Your child. I pray tonight for all the kids who can't think as quickly as I can.

October 10

Jesus, when You lived on earth, did You ever eat an apple? They are really fun to eat and crunch when you bite into them. And they taste good, too. I'm glad You made apples.

March 24

Help me to enjoy giving You
my offering. I don't have lots
of money to give You, but You
care more about me being
a cheerful giver. The next
time I drop my coins
in the offering plate,
remind me to smile.

October 9

My blankets feel so nice and warm, and I like to pull the covers up real high. Thanks, God, for covering me with Your love, all nice and warm.

March 25

There are a whole bunch of tiny islands way out in the ocean, Lord, where people live who don't know who You are. When they look up into the stars at night, help them to start looking for You.

October 8

Dear Lord, I remember being at a birthday party once and feeling jealous because my friend got a neat gift. It was something I really wanted. I'm sorry. Help me to be happy for my friends instead of thinking about myself.

March 26

Jesus, thank You for reminding us that You died for us. You remind us through communion. I don't really understand communion, so would You help me?

October 7

Help me to keep from talking back to Mom or Dad tomorrow, Lord. They deserve kind words from me.

March 27

The mind is a fantastic thing, Lord. With my mind I can think up all kinds of neat things to do and games to play. Thank You for my imagination (and may the things that I think make You happy).

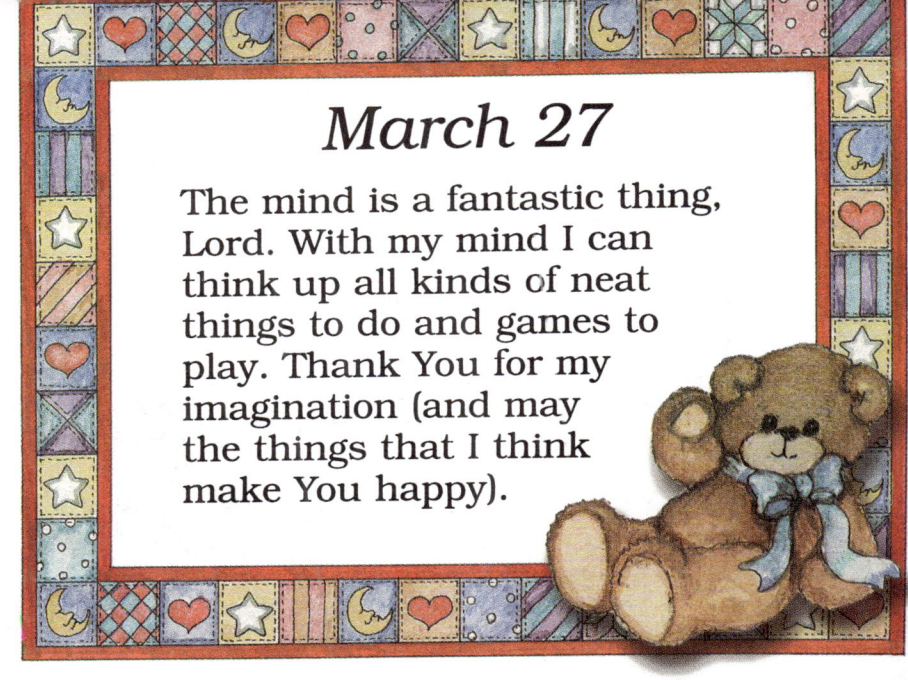

October 6

Sometimes I'm amazed
at the thoughts I can think.
What's really amazing is that
You know every single one
of them. Lord, help me
to think the kinds
of thoughts that
make You happy.

March 28

You had a good idea when You made the wind. Sometimes when it roars like a lion, I want to hide under the blankets. When the wind blows softly, it makes me feel all warm and nice inside. The wind is wonderful. Thanks, God.

October 5

October is an interesting month, God. It's so different from all the other times of the year. I'm glad You made October so windy and wonderful and colorful.

March 29

Thank You for writing to me.
There are lots of words in Your
letter to me (the Bible) that
I can't read or understand
yet, but I know Your
Word tells me that You
will always love and
forgive me.

October 4

Will I get married someday, Lord? If I do, I pray that the person I marry will love You. I hope we have lots of fun together.

March 30

It's hard to understand how Your disciple Peter could say he wasn't Your friend just before You died. Help me to always say that I'm Your friend.

October 3

Lord, wouldn't it be neat if I could trade houses with my friends! I wonder what it would be like to have my best friend's bedroom. Then again...I think I'll stay right where I am. I like my house, Lord.

March 31

I love the gifts You give, Lord.
Gifts of health and play,
friends and family, and even
sunshine and rainbows.
I think the gifts You give
are even better than
birthday presents!

October 2

Sometimes it's hard to make peace when other kids are fighting. But I think You want me to be a peacemaker, God. I'll be happy if I help to make peace because the Bible says, "Blessed are the peacemakers."

April 1

Today was April Fool's Day.
I guess no one can play an
April Fool's joke on You
because You know everything.
Just think: I'm friends
with someone who
knows everything!

October 1

I'm glad that You made leaves so they would fall off the trees. It's neat the way they circle when they fall—falling leaves look like they're dancing!

April 2

Cousins are neat friends, Lord. It would be great if I could spend lots of time with them. Help my cousins to know You and love You too, Jesus.

September 30

Lord, of all the people in the world, You chose brothers and sisters for me to be closest to. Thank You for making them part of my family. And please help us to be extra close.

April 3

Your words are a "lamp unto my feet," Lord. Would You shine Your light brightly on my path so I can see the way You want me to go? Thanks!

September 29

The farmers are gathering their harvest right now, Lord. I know it takes a lot of hard work to bring in all the grain and vegetables. I pray that they will have a good harvest!

April 4

Lord, I hope my family can go on vacation this summer. It's fun to do things I can't do around home and see new places. It's great to enjoy the world You created.

September 28

Joy and peace are gifts that You give to people who love You. I want to reach out to You and take Your gifts of joy and peace. What great gifts, God!

April 5

Jesus, the prayer You gave to the disciples says, "Your kingdom come, Your will be done on earth as it is in heaven." Lord, I hope people on earth will catch on to all the great ideas You have up there in heaven.

September 27

My bicycle is the best for getting around really fast. I feel like I can go as fast as the wind on my bike. Thanks for keeping me safe when I'm riding it.

April 6

God, I think that You probably like to hear praise choruses at the end of the day, so I think I'm going to sing You one right now!

September 26

Lord, tomorrow I want to do a Servant Surprise. That means I'd like to be Your servant and do something special tomorrow as a surprise for someone. I love being Your servant, Lord.

April 7

Jesus, I wish they would have made crayons when You were a little boy. They have all kinds of super colors. They must have 15 shades of pink now. People are beginning to catch on to how wonderful Your colors are!

September 25

Lord, I love the noses of little ponies. They're real soft and feel cozy and warm. I like ponies. And I like touching their noses. Thanks for coming up with the idea of...ponies!

April 8

I like holding my Bible
close to my heart, Lord.
But it's even better when
Your Word is *in* my heart.
Help me to do a good
job of memorizing
verses.

September 24

I love to sing and shout and sometimes even bark like a dog or cluck like a chicken. Just think, You gave us vocal chords so we could shout and sing! Thank You that I have a voice.

April 9

The farmers are planting lots of seeds right now, and they are hoping that lots of things grow. I pray for the sun to shine and the rain to fall on the new little seeds so that all of us will have food to eat.

September 23

Blue jeans are the best, Lord. I have a favorite pair of blue jeans that I love wearing all the time. Thanks for giving us comfortable clothes like...jeans!

April 10

I like it when I draw something and someone says "Wow, that's great!" I think tomorrow I'll draw something for my pastor. And by the way, God, tonight I pray for my pastor.

September 22

Lord, there are Muslims and Buddhists who don't know the truth about You. Please help them to find You, the One true God.

April 11

Zillions of people all over the world are praying, God, and I like to think that my little prayer is being added to theirs. Together, all our prayers make a wonderful difference in the world. So tonight, I pray for all the others who are praying, too.

September 21

I don't think about it often, but we'd be in big trouble if You didn't make air for us to breathe. Thank You that You did. Please remind me that each time I breathe it's because of You. I pray, too, that the air in our town will stay clean.

April 12

I like it when my friends come over and play. It's like a party. I wish I could be with my friends all the time...and one day in heaven, I will. Thank You for the biggest party of all that's coming real soon.

September 20

I know you'll be really busy in heaven, Jesus, but someday I'd like to go for a walk beside the crystal sea, just You and me. I really love You and want to be with You.

April 13

When I get tempted to do or say bad things, help me to remember, God, that with You, saying "no" can be easy.

September 19

Lord, I pray for the crossing guards at schools. They help a lot of kids cross streets and they protect them from traffic. I pray for *their* safety tonight.

April 14

There are soldiers across the ocean who are feeling lonely, Lord. Would You help them not to feel so alone? Help them to remember that there are lots of people like me praying for them.

September 18

Cancer is a bad disease and many people are sick because of it. Tonight I pray for all the scientists and researchers who are looking for a cure for cancer. I hope they find one soon!

April 15

God, I think You must have smiled a lot when You made flowers. I don't know all of their names, but they sure look beautiful...and smell sweet!

September 17

MacDonalds is the neatest place for hamburgers! Thanks for a fun place where kids can just be...kids! And I pray for the people behind the counter who take the orders.

April 16

God, when I go to heaven I'm glad I won't wear an angel costume with white wings. Instead, I'll have a brand new body and I'll be able to jump and run like I do now— only better and faster. Thanks for heaven!

September 16

I pray for my babysitter.
She helps my parents and
she makes sure that I'm
taken care of when they
go out. My babysitter
is a good person and
I pray for her.

April 17

There must be lots of kids who have a parent in jail. I want to pray for those kids tonight, and I also want to pray for the parent in jail. Help make everything right in their family, Lord.

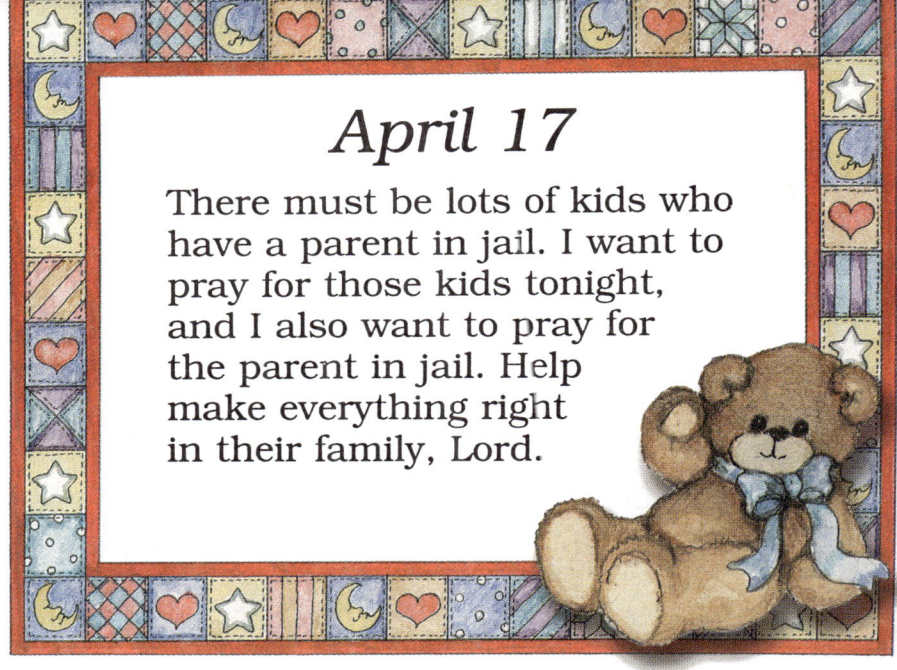

September 15

The Bible says that I am supposed to love You with all my heart and soul and mind and strength. Help me to love You with everything I've got.

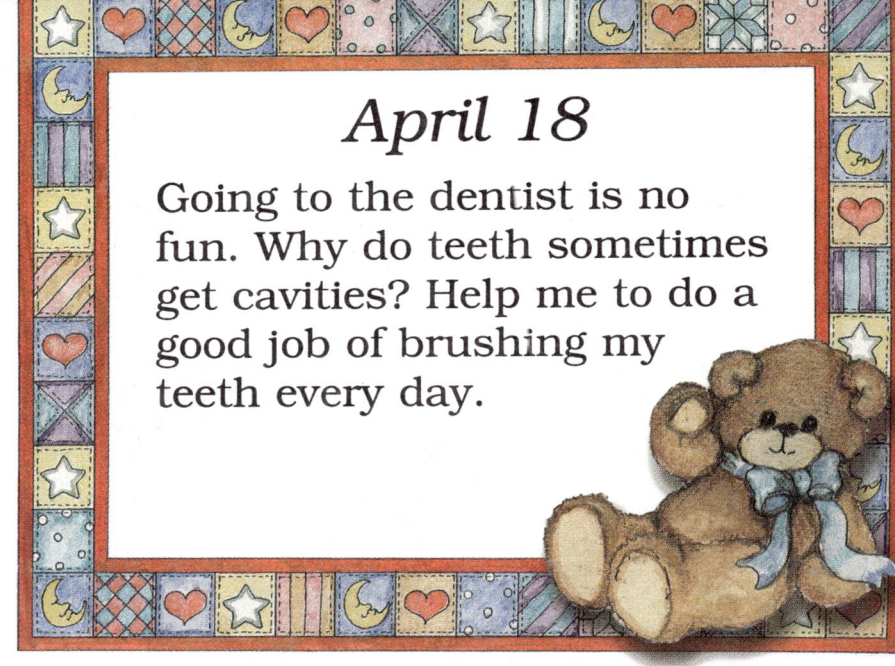

April 18

Going to the dentist is no fun. Why do teeth sometimes get cavities? Help me to do a good job of brushing my teeth every day.

September 14

God, tonight I pray that You would make me more like Jesus. I want to be a good helper to my parents and friendly to everyone around me. Thank You for making me like Jesus.

April 19

I like the story of David and Goliath, Lord. There are problems that seem big in my life, like Goliath. Sometimes I feel small when I look at them, like David must have felt. David conquered his big problem with Your help.... I can do the same!

September 13

I love my crayons and coloring books. Drawing is a lot of fun, and I like it when Dad or Mom puts one of my drawings up on the refrigerator. Thank You for teaching me how to draw.

April 20

God, when it's rainy,
help me to look
for rainbows.

September 12

God, I'm thankful that You filled my world with lots and lots of friends. I love having friends, each and every one of them. Remind me to tell my friends tomorrow that I think they're great!

April 21

Someday I might have a job like Mom or Dad. I pray that I will grow up to be a good worker and a good parent, too.

September 11

I *know* that You know where Israel is, Jesus. It's where You lived when You were a little boy! Now there's fighting there. Please protect the children!

April 22

Lord, I don't like it when I get sick—especially when my stomach is upset. But thank You for giving me someone as special as my mom to help me feel better.

September 10

A lot of kids are hurting because their moms and dads are going through divorce. Please put Your arms around these kids and hold them close to You. I pray that they will run to You...because You are their Hiding Place!

April 23

I'm glad You invented hugs, Lord. Neck hugs, tickle hugs, bear hugs, and squeezes of all shapes and sizes. Remind me to give at least three hugs to friends tomorrow. Thank You for hugs.

September 9

I love the game of hide-and-seek, Lord. It says in the Bible that You are my hiding place. That means I can run to You whenever I feel scared. Thank You for being a safe place for me to hide.

April 24

Lord, keep me from watching TV programs that teach things You don't like. Tell my heart when I should change the channel or turn off the TV.

September 8

Lord, I hear people say that You are the Alpha and Omega, the First and the Last, the Beginning and the End. You are everywhere all at the same time. Besides that, You know everything. God, You are...*awesome!*

April 25

There's a country we call India where elephants and tigers and Brahman bulls live. Millions of people are crowded together in India, and many of them are children who live in the streets and beg. I pray for the children of India tonight.

September 7

I would like to be more patient, Lord. So the next time things don't happen when I want them to, would You remind me to wait happily?

April 26

I don't know why it rains in April, Lord, but I'm glad it does. Whether it's soft drizzle or a thunder shower, rain is Your way of watering the earth.

September 6

The weather is beginning to turn cooler, and it reminds me that You are in charge of the seasons, God. I'm excited about the change in seasons. Thank You for the way You always make our world so interesting.

April 27

God, having You for my Father is the best thing that could have ever happened in my life. Thank You for letting me be in Your family.

September 5

Cousins are great, Lord!
They're a lot of fun—I wish
I saw them more often.
I want to pray for my
cousins tonight. Their
names are _____
_____.

April 28

Lord, I want to help people. Is there someone who needs my help? Please show that person to me so I can be a friend.

September 4

Lord, please be with the people who live next door on our left. I pray that they'll be safe and that they'll enjoy having us as their neighbors. Maybe we can make cookies for them this week!

April 29

It's sad when neat animals like dogs and rabbits die. Please help me to understand that it's a normal thing for animals to die and that I don't have to be sad.

September 3

Lord, please be with the people who live next door on our right. If they don't know You, I pray that our family will be good examples for them of what it means to be a Christian.

April 30

Jesus loves the little children, all the children of the world. Red and yellow, black and white, they are precious in His sight. Jesus loves the little children of the world.
(And that includes me. Thanks, Jesus!)

September 2

Dear God, please help me to find a hero I can look up to. Mom and Dad and my Sunday School teacher are heroes, but I'd like to have just one more. I want to learn something from a special hero.

May 1

Once in a while I pretend I'm blind. It's really a strange feeling, Lord. Help those who are blind all the time not to bump into things or feel bad about not being able to see the faces of people they love.

September 1

Lord, it's hard to see over the heads of people in front of me at church. I would like to be like Zacchaeus in the tree so that I could see what's going on. I'm so glad I don't have to be tall to be loved by You.

May 2

It would be so much fun for me to be able to drive our car. Sometimes it seems hard to wait until I'm a teenager. Thanks for our car and keeping us safe on the road. Thanks for seat belts, too!

August 31

Jesus, some day soon I'll start school. I feel excited and scared all at once. Would You please help me to like it and to make new friends?

May 3

Dear Lord, I've saved some money in my bank. Help me to know how to spend it. And help me to know how to use my allowance, too.

August 30

Thank You for taking care of me when I'm asleep. The Bible says that You never sleep and that You've always been and always will be awake. Wow! I wish I could do that!

May 4

Lots of music is fun, Lord, but some music doesn't make You happy. Teach me which kinds of music You like.

August 29

Lord, help me to eat the kinds of foods that are good for me— and not too much candy or ice cream. Thank You for food that will make me strong and healthy even though it may not taste the way I like.

May 5

Jesus, I hear people say that they want to get to know You better. Sometimes I feel like saying, "God, would You like to get to know me better?" Help me to remember that You already know *me* inside and out!

August 28

God, thank You for all the park rangers who take care of parks and picnic areas. Thank You that they keep these wonderful places safe for families like mine.

May 6

Lord, the prayer You gave to the disciples says, "Give us this day our daily bread." Thank You for giving us all the good things on our plates tonight at dinner.

August 27

I wonder what my mansion in heaven will look like? I hope it has a big playroom so I can invite over my friends. Jesus, I'm so glad I'll finally get to see You...my *best* friend.

May 7

God, I know that You made me,
but I also know that You haven't
finished making me yet. You
want to keep making me into
a better person. I pray that
I will work along with You
so I can be the very
best for You.

August 26

I think grandmothers and grandfathers are one of Your best ideas, because they are kind and loving to little kids. Thank You for being kind and loving to grandparents.

May 8

You know what it's like to be in a storm at sea, Lord. Please be with all the people in big ships out on the ocean— especially where there are storms.

August 25

Lord, my heart is wide open tonight. Would You please fill it up with joy?

May 9

Thank You for time to go to bed and sleep. When I sleep, my body has a chance to rest. I think it's fantastic that You made the nighttime so that we could go to sleep.

August 24

Some people think humans used to be monkeys many, many years ago. The Bible says You made people. I believe You. Thank You for making people and animals so different.

May 10

I love to read stories from Your Bible, Lord. That way I can learn about the miracles and the good things You have done for people. I love Your Word, God.

August 23

I have a favorite uncle, Lord, and I want to pray for him tonight. Please bless my uncle and give him a great year. His name is

_____.

May 11

There are lots of words to describe You, Lord, but I'm thinking of one special word right now that describes You best and it's this:

_____!

August 22

Thank You for the Holy Spirit. I don't always understand everything the Holy Spirit does, but the Bible says that He comforts me and guides me. Thanks, Lord, for Your Spirit!

May 12

The earth looks like it's going to burst with all the brand new flowers and the trees with their little green leaves. Spring is in full bloom... and it's great! Thank You that Spring is finally here, Lord.

August 21

Picnics are fun! I love to eat wedges of watermelon on paper plates. Thank You for picnics. (Maybe we can go on one soon.)

May 13

Thank You for my mom's hands. Her hands do so many things for me. They touch me, they clean my clothes, they make my supper, and they clap when I do something she likes.

August 20

Russia is a great big country. For many years the people who live there were not allowed to have churches. Thank You, Lord, that today the people in Russia can worship You. Help them to find peace in You.

May 14

Help me to take good care of Your earth. Please remind me to put my trash in wastebaskets—even my crumpled up gum wrappers. And please remind others to take good care of the earth, too.

August 19

My Bible is so special to me, God. I feel like You wrote it just for me. My Bible has lots of answers in it. It's like having a treasure!

May 15

When I ride my bike through my neighborhood, Lord, it's neat to look at all the houses and think about the people who live there. I pray for my neighborhood tonight and all the families in their homes.

August 18

Grownups talk about having a good attitude, Lord. It's hard to understand but I guess they mean being happy about things and obeying with a smile. I want to have a good attitude and obey with a smile, Jesus.

May 16

I know You care about China, Lord, because millions of people live there and it's very crowded. The government doesn't like Christians very much, so please help the little churches to grow and be strong.

August 17

Lord, I know a person who has a disability and I think he needs my prayer. Would You help this person to feel important and stay strong and healthy? Thank You, Lord. The person's name is

_____.

May 17

Thanks for music, Lord. It makes me smile in my heart when I hear my favorite song on the radio. I think I'll sing to You right now.

August 16

Lord, the prayer You gave Your disciples says, "For Yours is the kingdom, and the power and the glory forever and ever. Amen." Everything is Yours and You are Super with a capital "S"!

May 18

Everybody gets angry, even me. Help me to do the right thing even when I'm angry. Instead of getting mad at somebody, can I just talk to You about it?

August 15

God, You had a good idea when You made bugs like fireflies and caterpillars and grasshoppers. Are lady bugs really ladies and do praying mantises really pray?

May 19

Every now and then I lose a tooth, Lord. It's fun to think about what all of my grown-up teeth are going to look like. By the way, I really like the Tooth Fairy story, especially the part about the nickels and quarters.

August 14

Sometimes when I pray I feel like I'm doing all the talking and not giving You a chance to talk to me. Do You have anything that You want to tell me tonight? I'll be quiet and listen.

May 20

Lord, when You were a little boy, did You have a yo-yo? What did You play with when You were a kid? I'm glad that You think playtime is important. I have an idea that in heaven we will have lots of time to play. Thanks for playtime!

August 13

Dear God, my favorite verse
from the Bible is _____.
I just want to tell You my
verse tonight so that
You'll know that I'm
learning Your Word.

May 21

Lord, I know You want families to love each other. Help families to stick together through hard times so that they will be strong in Your love. Help families everywhere, Lord.

August 12

My church does a lot of good things to help people. It helps prisoners, older people and disabled people, and people in hospitals and nursing homes. I want to pray for my church...it's really *Your* church, isn't it?

May 22

Lord, I love it when the sun shines on my shoulders. Thank You for the sunshine that keeps us warm.

August 11

Taking a bath is a good thing—and sometimes it's lots of fun because of all the soap bubbles. Thank You for washing me on the inside, Lord. Thank You for giving me a clean heart.

May 23

Lord, help me not to miss
a chance to do something
nice for other people...
like give them a
special smile.

August 10

The Bible talks about wisdom, Lord. Wisdom means learning about right and wrong. Please make me wise, Lord.

May 24

I can't believe how many names You have! Father, God, Jesus, Lord, Creator, Savior... there must be thousands! And You deserve each one because You're the greatest!

August 9

I'm glad you made dads, Lord.
Help all fathers everywhere to
be kind and strong, honest
and brave, and to love their
families. I love my dad.
Thank You for giving
him to me, and me
to him.

May 25

Thank You for soft, chocolate chip cookies fresh out of the oven and for mozzarella cheese that oozes off my pizza. Thank You for food that tastes good and feels good in my mouth.

August 8

Lord, thank You for my mother's hands. She shows me she loves me with her hands. She uses them to clean things and cook and even dress me. Thank You for that, God.

May 26

Thank You for strawberries,
raspberries, blueberries,
huckleberries, blackberries...
and every other kind
of berry that makes
summertime taste
so good!

August 7

I love a hot summer day, Lord.
And I love walking barefoot so
I can feel the grass and dirt
on my feet. I love splashing
in a stream and taking a
nap under a big tree.
Thanks, God, for the
season of summer.

May 27

I like my bedroom so much, Lord. It has all my special things in it and it's a safe place to be. Thank You for all my things on the shelves and pictures hanging on the wall. I like to pray in my bedroom!

August 6

There's an older person who lives nearby, and sometimes I think that person must feel lonely. I want to pray that You will show extra special love to this friend. My friend is _____.

May 28

Thank you for rules, Lord.
Rules aren't always fun
but You said rules help
us to grow and keep
us safe.

August 5

I love lemonade and Popsicles and snow cones in all kinds of flavors. Thank You, God, for making things that taste cold and sweet. Especially on a hot day.

May 29

I like the story of the battle of Jericho where the walls came a-tumbling down. Walking around the city so many times probably seemed silly to the people. But they obeyed and look what happened! I want to do whatever You want, even if it looks silly.

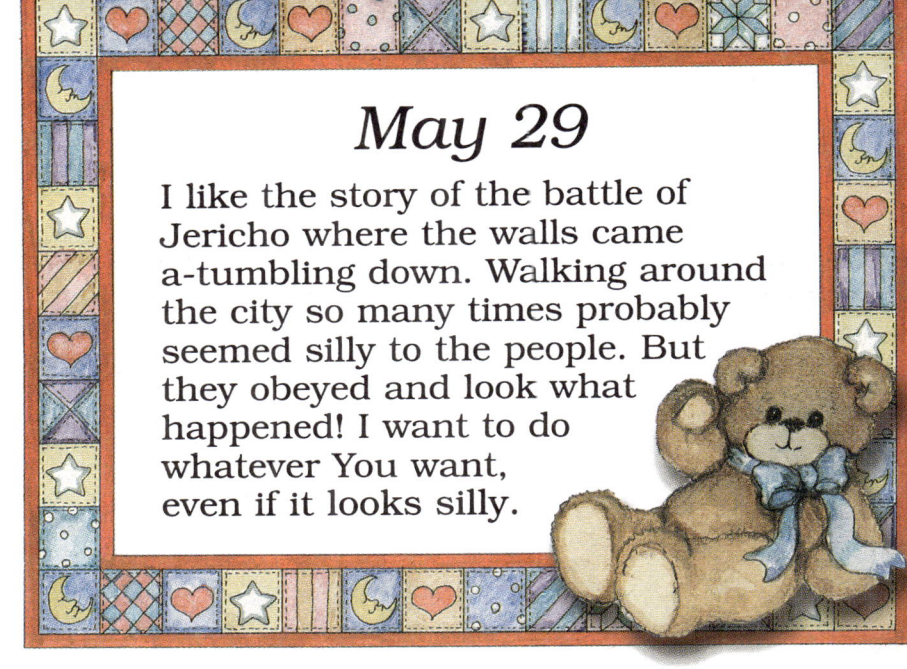

August 4

The Bible says that one day I'll ride a big white horse with You (You told me so in Revelation 19:14)! That's neat! I can't wait to be a part of the armies of heaven, Lord. Come quickly...I'd love to ride horses with You!

May 30

I'd like to invent a new color, Lord. It's the color that describes the light in heaven. I think I'll call this color _____. I can't wait to see what it actually looks like.

August 3

Jesus, when You were a little boy, were You afraid of the lightning and thunder? Probably not. But You know what? I'm sometimes afraid. Help me not to be scared of things that You're in control of...like thunder!

May 31

Psalm 82:4 says, "Rescue the weak and needy." Will You please do that tonight, Lord? There are a lot of people in our town who need Your love. Thank You for caring.

August 2

Sometimes when I lose
things, I forget to ask You
to help me to find them.
I promise the next time
I lose something, I'll
come running to
You first for help.

June 1

Summer will soon be here.
Oh, Lord, that makes me
feel really happy inside.
Thanks for making
summer!

August 1

God, thank You for colors.
They make our world so
interesting and beautiful.
We use Your colors to do all
kinds of crazy things—like
make blue Jell-O. I'm
glad You thought to
create color!

June 2

Jesus, I don't think they had bubble gum when you were a little kid. I wonder if You know how fun it is to chew and how good it tastes? Thanks for fun things like bubbles popping and sticky gum all over my lips.

July 31

Camels are funny looking, Lord. Where did You ever come up with the idea for an animal like that! Thanks for having such wonderful, funny ideas.

June 3

Waiting is hard, Lord.
Whether it's waiting in line
or waiting for vacation to
come, I know You want me
to learn how to wait.
Thanks for the patience
it teaches me.

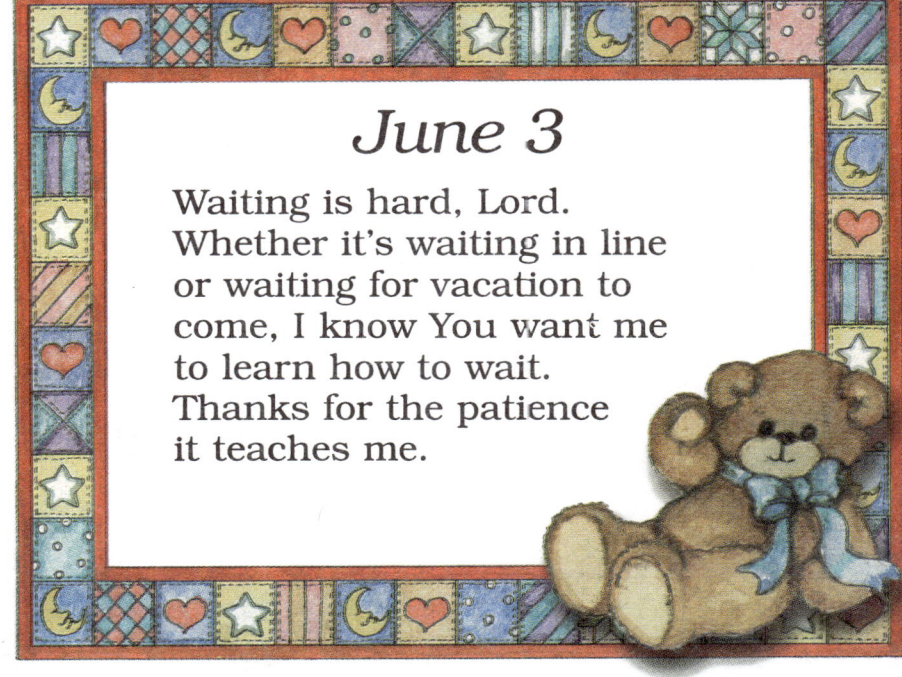

July 30

It's so neat to pray to You every night, Jesus. Thanks for meeting me here by my bed to listen to what I have to say every night.

June 4

I like watching my shadow when it's a sunny day. The Bible says that we can run for cover in Your shadow and You will protect us. I'm glad Your shadow is always there, no matter whether it's sunny or rainy. Thank You for protecting me.

July 29

Some days I feel lonely, Lord.
Especially when I don't see
any of my friends. I wonder
what they're doing. I'm glad
You know all about my
friends. Would You
please take care of
them tomorrow?

June 5

I'm glad that because Jesus died on the cross, I can go to heaven. But I want lots of others to be in heaven with me, so I pray tonight that more people would ask Jesus into their hearts and be saved.

July 28

Sometimes on warm summer nights I can hear the crickets and frogs. It's a nice sound that makes me feel happy inside. Thank You, God, for frogs and crickets and all the other wonderful summertime sounds like _____.

June 6

Jesus, they say that You live in my heart. But sometimes the space in my heart feels very small and You are so big. Would You please stretch my heart and make it bigger so I can love You more?

July 27

Thanks, God, for things like fans and air conditioners and cool breezes. They remind me that You are exactly what the Bible says You are: a cool shelter in the heat of the day.

June 7

Lord, I pray for all of the kids whose parents don't have jobs. Let them know that You are taking care of them. And please help their parents to be able to work again.

July 26

Lord, I pray for our mail carrier tonight. Every day he brings us letters. I hope he's happy about his job because we sure do like to get mail. Maybe I can do something nice for him sometime.

June 8

Do I pray funny, Lord? I don't sound like my pastor or other grownups. On second thought, there's no such thing as a strange prayer to You. You enjoy it when kids come and talk to You.

July 25

Sometimes cars and houses have burglar alarms on them so that people don't steal. I wish Adam and Eve hadn't sinned so people wouldn't steal things and we wouldn't have to even lock our doors. I pray that our house will stay safe.

June 9

People say that You never forget, but I don't agree. There is one thing You do forget and that's my sin. Thank You, Lord, for forgetting the sins that I have told You about.

July 24

I'm glad the Bible is true. It contains no lies. God, help me to always tell the truth and to never, ever lie. I know it's very important to obey You, God. Thank You for reminding me.

June 10

I want to be full of love, joy, peace, and all the other fruit of the Spirit, Lord. I want to be a bowl full of Your fruit!

July 23

God, it's fantastic that when I put my hand over my heart I can feel it beating. Tha-thump, tha-thump. Thank You for my heart.

June 11

Lord, the prayer You gave Your disciples says, "Forgive us our debts as we forgive our debtors." Help me to forgive others the same way You forgive me. That's a lot of forgiving, but with You I can do it.

July 22

I love the stars in the summertime. It's amazing that You know the names of all the stars—zillions of them! Thank You that You know *my* name, too. Let me be a star for You, Jesus.

June 12

I pray for all the farmers in the country. They have to work really hard, and sometimes the weather gets so bad that nothing will grow. Help them to trust You for just the right amount of rain and sun.

July 21

You talked to the prophet Samuel when he was just a little boy. Sometimes I wish my ears could hear Your voice. For now, let me listen carefully to You by reading Your Bible.

June 13

Jesus, there are a whole lot of little wars going on all over the world in countries everywhere. The children are being hurt most. Please protect them.

July 20

Thank You for books, Lord. We wouldn't be able to learn things without them. There are so many great books to look at and read. My favorite book is _____.

June 14

Lord, please bless my father tonight. He has lots to do and so many things to think about. I really love my dad and I would like it if You would show him tonight how much You love him.

July 19

I feel sad and guilty whenever
I'm punished and it makes me
wonder...Jesus, how did You
feel when You were punished
for us on the cross? Thank
You for going through
something so awful
for me.

June 15

God, it's amazing when You look real, real close at a rose petal. It feels so soft and it has little tiny veins and it smells like perfume. It's incredible to think that You dreamed up the idea of making roses...and their petals.

July 18

Dear Lord, I don't like nightmares. They make me upset. Please help me to have fun dreams about pools filled with Jell-O or getting to spend a whole year at Disney World.

June 16

The Bible says we only need faith the size of a mustard seed. That's about the smallest seed You made! Please help me to have faith in You.

July 17

Jesus, it's neat to think that Joseph, Your dad down here on earth, probably let You use a hammer and nails and wood. When You made things, did You think about making planets and stars? Thank You for making me!

June 17

I like it a lot when people say I've done a good job. Please help me to do the same to other kids so that they'll feel great.

July 16

Help me to be like a bee, Lord—always busy and always sweet. Help me to be like a dog, Lord—always happy and always Your best friend. Help me to be like a horse, Lord—always strong and always quick to do what You want.

June 18

It's wonderful to think about how You kept Daniel safe in the lion's den. I'm glad that when I go to the zoo, there are big bars between the lions and me. You kept Daniel safe from danger. Thanks for keeping me safe from danger, too!

July 15

Jesus, what kinds of chores did You do when You were my age? Tomorrow, help me to do the things I have to do around my house with a smile.

June 19

Lord, it seems like a lot of people get sick with AIDS. Could I ask You to help doctors find a cure for AIDS? Thank You.

July 14

Lord, You had a great idea when You made jungles. I love the tigers and the monkeys. But lots of people live in jungles, too. Help missionaries to reach the tribes in the jungles.

June 20

Lord, once in a while I do something careless—like spilling my milk or tripping as I walk. Remind me to be careful. I'm so glad that I'll be stronger and do things better when I'm older.

July 13

Lord, the prayer You gave Your disciples says, "Lead us not into temptation, but deliver us from evil." Thank You that You do this every day, Lord. Because of You, the devil can't touch me!

June 21

I love it when my back gets scratched or rubbed. It feels so good. Jesus, help me to do things for other people to make them feel good, too.

July 12

They say that sticks and stones may break my bones, but names will never hurt me. I don't believe that—names hurt! When kids say bad things about me, help me to run to You. You can heal the hurt.

June 22

God, I love it when the moon is big and white and full. The moon makes the nighttime so bright and beautiful. Help me to glow with Your love when things get dark around me.

July 11

Lord, lots of things are happening at my church. I want to pray for my Sunday School teacher tonight and all the kids in my class.

June 23

I'm glad that You are a Heavenly Father who is always kind and loving. But I'm also glad that You are a Heavenly Father who disciplines Your children as good fathers should. Thank You for being my Father in heaven.

July 10

I'm sure glad that You invented water, Jesus. Swimming is fun. I guess You splashed Your feet in a stream when You were a little boy. It feels good, doesn't it! People make swimming pools...but You make the water. Thanks!

June 24

It hurts when other kids tease me, Lord. Help me not to be mean back to them, but instead, help me to show them love and forgiveness. That's what You would do. Help me to do the same.

July 9

Sometimes when I hurt myself
playing, I cry so hard that I
almost forget about You.
Help me to remember that
You don't leave me when
I hurt. Your love is like
a big Band-Aid!

June 25

Tonight I want to promise You something, Lord. If I see a butterfly tomorrow, it will be a reminder to think of You. This summer send lots of butterflies my way.

July 8

When I think of really great
vegetables, I think of corn.
People make cornbread
and corn-on-the-cob
and popcorn. Yum!
Thanks, God,
for corn.

June 26

I like my pillow, Lord. It's soft and fluffy and just right for me. Thank You for caring for my comfort—even when I'm fast asleep on my pillow.

July 7

Was it hard for You to obey Your mom when You were a little boy, Jesus? Just like You, I want to do what's right. Help me to say "Yes!" with a smile when my mom tells me what to do.

June 27

Lord, the Bible says that one day in the future there's going to be a big supper in heaven. The table that everyone will sit around must be huge. Can I sit near You?

July 6

Jesus, I love You. And I love to listen to You. You are great and full of bright light. You are strong and powerful and gentle. You are the best, Jesus.

June 28

Dear Lord, please bless our garbage man. It seems like he's got a really dirty job, but it sure is important. Without him, our garage would be full of garbage and our house would stink! Do You think I could do something for him?

July 5

I guess that You probably
invented things like toys and
puzzles and hide-and-seek and
somersaults. I love it that You
planned for children to play.
Thank You for giving me
time to play...and
friends to play with!

June 29

Cleaning my room is lots of work, Lord. But with Your help I can do it.

July 4

I love fireworks, God!
I love the way they fill the
summer sky with pretty
colors and light. They
make me want to
celebrate!

June 30

You already know this, Jesus, but there are old people who live in places called nursing homes. Some of them are sick and lonely. Please comfort them tonight so they can get a good night's sleep.

July 3

I'm impressed, God! I've been thinking about Your sunsets and the hundreds of animals and birds and flowers You made. You do great work!

July 1

I don't suppose there was an ice cream shop in Nazareth when You were a boy, but somehow I'm sure you know all about them. Thanks for ice cream—especially my favorite flavor, which is _____!

July 2

Summertime means vacation. Lots of people will be traveling in cars and planes. Would You please keep them safe? Keep my family safe on our vacation, too.